F**K THE
ESTABLISHMENT

F**K THE ESTABLISHMENT

101
ways to get
your voice heard and
change the world

SEVEN DIALS

First published in Great Britain in 2019 by Seven Dials
An imprint of Orion Publishing Group Ltd
Carmelite House, 50 Victoria Embankment, London, EC4Y 0DZ

An Hachette UK Company

1 3 5 7 9 10 8 6 4 2

Text © Orion Publishing Group Ltd 2019

Illustrations by Emanuel Santos

A CIP catalogue record for this book is
available from the British Library.

Hardback ISBN: 9781841883663
Ebook ISBN: 9781841883670

Printed and bound by CPI Group (UK) Ltd, Croydon, CR0 4YY

MIX
Paper from
responsible sources
FSC® C104740

www.orionbooks.co.uk

CONTENTS

INTRODUCTION

What's wrong with the Establishment?

Good question, we have no idea. The same thing that's always being wrong with them, we suspect: all too often they are people who are out of touch, have limited experience in what they're talking about, or only have their own interests at heart.

But that's the wrong question to be asking – because the answer isn't easily identifiable and therefore the problem isn't tangible or fixable. What this book should really be called is *FORGET the Establishment*. They are only important in that they might be the obstacle you need to overcome in achieving change, which is exactly what this book is all about.

Can I really change the world?

It feels like such a big ask, doesn't it? Even saying the words makes us feel tired. It feels gargantuan and unwieldy. So, first things first, the world doesn't have to be the entire planet: it is *your* world, and that might be your village, your hometown, your new town, your school, your workplace or your country. If it genuinely is the whole world, that's ace too, but starting with one of the above and then going from there will make your task easier.

Second, you need a clear goal. What is it about the world that you want to change? Your cause might be something to do with health, education, green issues, happiness, economic success, social harmony, the list goes on. Whatever it is, write it down here:

....

Now you've got this goal (and you're already reading this book so you must have passion) you're ready to dive into the 101 tips, tricks and ideas kept safe in this book that have been tried and tested by activists before you. But before we begin, let's get some perspective . . .

Why is the world getting worse?

The world is no worse today than it ever has been. Let's not be the purveyors of fake news and kid ourselves that it is any worse now than it was in yesteryear — and hopefully this knowledge can make us all feel a little better. The twentieth century, for example, was positively a shit-show.

The Holocaust, the A-bombs in Hiroshima and Nagasaki, the napalm and Agent Orange atrocities in Vietnam, the genocides in Cambodia, Rwanda and plenty of other places, Apartheid, the rape crimes in the Bosnian War, dictators like Pinochet – if you live in a country that did not commit or facilitate crimes against humanity in the twentieth century, you are in the minority and may throw yourselves a party. An estimated 142 MILLION people (that's roughly the entire population of Russia, or all of Selena Gomez's Instagram followers) died due to wars between 1900 and 2000.[1] And let's not even get started on the amount of animals that went extinct.

BUT, on the flip side, the twentieth century was pretty great too, hey? Albert Einstein came up with his Theory of Relativity, women's suffrage spread, a man stood on the moon, new vaccines were discovered, gay rights increased, the Pill was conceived, segregation in the US ended, the internet was invented, the Oreo created, the Beatles existed, *Harry Potter* was published – and a good portion of the terrible things? They came to an end. If every action has an equal and opposite reaction, whilst things got really shady, there were also plenty of things to celebrate.

The point? The mood in the world right now isn't good. Some of us might be feeling let down by our governments, or in a country where the economy is slipping off a cliff, or watching our education, legal and health systems crumble; some of us might be watching the rich and poor divide increase, or feeling racial tensions rise, or keeping track of the new wars breaking out, or losing sleep over the large country of plastic floating in the Pacific Ocean (and as sure as Winter is Coming, so is climate change). In most western countries (save maybe Norway) if you were born between 1981 and 2000, then you are the first generation to be worse off than your parents in living memory. It's very annoying.[2]

But just like the twentieth century, there are so many positives attached to this time we are living through and so many people who are already making a difference to the issues we face. We mustn't feel defeated or hopeless. And one of those plenty of positives? You and I have never had so much opportunity to make change 🙌 .

A change is gonna come

Since its inception in 2007, the petition website Change.Org has had over 270 million users across 196 countries.[3] And in big cities across the world, you can't swing a cat on a weekend without hitting a protester nowadays. You will no doubt have heard of the Women's March on 21 January 2017, when a reported 673 marches involving all seven continents took place. Let's take a moment to celebrate just how cool that is 👏 .

Depending on where you live, you might *not* have heard of the annual Invasion Day rallies in Australia, which grew from 400 people in 2015 to over 100,000 in 2019; or the one million schoolchildren in America who led an anti-gun protest in 2018; or the thousands who gathered across Brazil after the murder of Rio de Janeiro city councillor Marielle Franco; or the tens of thousands who marched in Venezuela against President Maduro. It certainly feels like there have been more protests and signatures on petitions in the twenty-first century than ever before. Is it because there are more causes to rally for or against? Absolutely not, and I'm sure with the magic of hindsight sociologists and historians will find plenty of reasons to explain this sheer amount of resistance. But what's *facilitating* this rise? Undoubtedly it's the internet. Avaaz, the campaigning equivalent of David (in its underdog championing) *and* Goliath (in its giant proportions), has over 50 million members worldwide and has achieved incredible things, from being the major driver behind the Paris Climate Agreement to marking out an area the size of Germany and Italy combined for ocean conservation projects.[4] The internet has its downsides, but if you can utilise its power, you can bring a group of people together more quickly and in greater numbers than ever before. And if there's one thing you need to effect change, it's people power.

Here's just a few things people power has achieved:

🤛 In the late 80s, protests were sweeping eastern Europe and change was in the air. In Berlin, where a wall had divided east from west for over 25 years, Berliners showed up in large numbers at the border. The men guarding the wall, who had also heard of the revolutions elsewhere in Europe, couldn't control them and so started to let them pass from one side to the other. Shortly after, the wall was pulled down.

The 2014 Sunflower Student Movement in Taiwan saw students and civic groups protest against a trade pact with China by occupying the country's legislative chamber. The issue stemmed from the fact the ruling party had ignored a previous agreement that the trade pact should receive a clause-by-clause review with the opposition. There were many political outcomes resulting from the protests, not least that the trade agreement with China has never been ratified in Taiwanese legislature.

In Germany in February and March 1943, the non-Jewish wives and relatives of Jewish men who had been arrested decided to protest outside the prison where the men were awaiting deportation. The Rosenstrasse Protest as it came to be known was the only mass public demonstration against the deportation of Jews under the Nazis, and incredibly it was successful: the men were released and allowed to go home.

Is change really that simple?

Yes, and no. You've got to be clever with how you use people power. Protests CAN work: the French are experts, and you can find success stories all over the world, such as the student protests in Germany which saw the scrapping of university tuition fees back in 2013. But then you have examples like the worldwide protests against the Iraq War back in 2003: an estimated six to eleven million people across 60 countries marched, yet the war happened anyway. Making a protest's cause stick requires more than just numbers, something this book is going to give you tips on. But people power isn't just about protests – it's about understanding who you're up against, it's about finding weaknesses to chip away at, it's about having numbers, but not random numbers: numbers who have skills, or insider knowledge, or bargaining power.

Success is always going to be based on variables, for example your own skills, the skills of others around you, the mood and situational circumstances at the time – and sometimes the sparks you need to make something catch fire don't quite come together. But like everything in life, you can learn certain things to make success a lot more likely. Did you know that Rosa Parks learned to be a campaigner? She trained at a centre for civil rights activists called the Highlander Folk School, and had already been part of the civil rights movement for ten years before she refused to give up her seat on that bus. As brilliant a feat as it was, she wasn't suddenly inspired to take that action – it had been strategically planned.

You can change the world

Always remember that you have multiple things in common with Rosa – and Nelson Mandela, and Gandhi and the rest of them. Like them, you are an ordinary person born to an ordinary family. They also played, slept, went through puberty, cried, wet the bed, ate food, had to poo and probably got nervous. (Not in that order.) 99.9 per cent of your DNA is exactly the same as theirs was. And if they could change the world, why can't you?

You already effect change all the time – every day, on a daily basis. Forget any 'big issues' at stake for a minute and think of all the choices you've made today: the phone calls or emails or messages you sent initiating plans or giving advice or spelling out instructions; the things you bought from a shop that help pay the staff's wages and contribute to the company owner's profits; the healthy (or unhealthy) meal you cooked for yourself or for your family; thanking the bus driver when you got to your stop; getting annoyed with your energy company's customer service team; the hours you put in at school or at work.

Now imagine you DIDN'T do any of it, that all the

choices you made today that affected other people's lives never happened. The history you affected for each of those people would be different. History is not made by men in their ivory towers, though it might feel that way. In fact, to quote Alan Bennett's *The History Boys,* the beauty of history is that it's 'just one fucking thing after another.'[5] If you think of it like that you can shift your perspective to see that it's not some mystical, untouchable, mammoth thing that happened in the past, it is just a bunch of small things that happen, and continue to happen – which makes it feel far more achievable to grapple with and create. It shouldn't be heralded or worshipped or owned by a small group of people, it belongs to every single person on this planet who ever took one step forward or spoke aloud or made another person feel something. We are all creating history, because history is just one. fucking. thing. after. another.

Now that's settled, let's start making it, shall we?

WORK

IT,

BABY

(aka get your attitude in gear)

#1 You got roots

When you first decide you want to make change, it can feel like you're floating in the sea with nothing below you, whilst you struggle to keep your head above the water. Never forget you are actually standing on foundations that have been built since the beginning of time – you're on the battlements of a castle. Don't feel alone, or let anyone else feel that way either; no matter what your cause is you are treading in the footsteps of the Suffragettes, the abolitionists, the Indian Independence movement and thousands more.

#2 Campaigning's not just for Christmas

Democracy doesn't stop at the ballot box and don't let anyone tell you otherwise. The Oxford Dictionary defines democracy as 'a system of government by the whole population or all the eligible members of a state, typically through elected representatives.' Yes we elect representatives, but the key part of this sentence is 'a system of government by the **WHOLE POPULATION**'. The power belongs to you – and if you don't feel like it does then you are not abiding by the rules of a democracy. The Oxford Dictionary also defines democracy as 'control of an organisation or group by the majority of its members'.[6] Enough said. Do not let the politicians just get on with it. If you're not continually telling them what you're thinking, they're not going to know.

#3 Own the narrative

It's fine to not like something, to say you don't like something and leave it there. People who drive too close behind you, people who jump the queue, mosquitoes that buzz in your ear while you're trying to sleep etc. But the problem with doing that with a societal issue or a policy is that you're the afterthought; you're trying to say no to something that's already in motion that doesn't belong to you. If you want to see proper change, you need to pull some of that power towards yourself and believe you can find the solutions to the problem at hand.

You'll find pushing your initiative down the hill is much easier than pushing their initiative back up it.

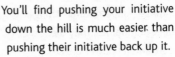

#4 Even your mental playing field

They're not big, you're not small. Power exists only if you believe in it. In the 90s hit film *Practical Magic*, Sandra Bullock says to Aidan Quinn that his sheriff's badge doesn't hold any *real* power; it only does because he believes it does. Through a similar thought process, in *Peter Pan*, the fairies are dying because children don't believe in them any more. Not to ruin a kid's book or anything, but this can be a brilliant metaphor for the status quo. Fairies don't exist, just like the status quo doesn't exist. Both are strange, supernatural things. When people don't believe in fairies, they die. Don't believe in the status quo, and its power dies too.

#5 Small is nimble

At the same time as shifting your perspective to not be scared of the power, also remember that it doesn't matter if your numbers aren't as large as theirs. Being a small group has its advantages. For the better part of a century, pirates around the world were outnumbered by thirty to one by the Royal Navy, yet they caused their fair share of trouble.[7]

#6 No one is born evil

Take a moment to consider that Darth Vader had real issues. Even Lord Voldemort did. Real people aren't born evil either, and people also don't *want* to be evil. Everyone has a moral compass, even if sometimes it's only there when peer pressure exposes it. The point is, don't make your opponent a Disney villain. You will be able to get to them; you just need to work out what matters to them and get speaking their language.

#7 Every vote counts

Get out of the mindset that you can't make a difference by voting – especially in times of political unrest when you don't know which way things are going to swing. (Politicians know this too – it's a time when they're more willing to listen to their constituents, something we should all use to our advantage.) In the UK general election of 2017, more young people than ever turned out to vote, stopping the ruling party who were tipped to win outright from getting a majority. Never forget that 'A mountain is composed of tiny grains of earth.'[8] To be a mountain, all those grains of earth need to turn up.

#8 Get organised

In the masterpiece of a movie that is *Chicken Run*, Mrs Tweedy doesn't take her revolting chickens seriously because she doesn't believe they can organise themselves. Whoever you're battling, they may well be a Mrs Tweedy and not take you seriously either, which gives you a head start and also gives you an opportunity to prove them wrong. You MUST be organised. This book will help you achieve this.

#9 Your cause matters

If you've ever watched *10 Things I Hate About You*, you might recall the scene where Julia Stiles talks diversion tactics with the teacher in charge of detention, then essentially flashing him so Heath Ledger can escape out the window. Don't let anyone flash you – it doesn't matter what else is happening in the world right now or if the power you're up against tells you there are larger issues they need to deal with: they are trying to use diversion tactics against you. Always remember that your goal is important too.

#10 Don't get scared

Depending on what change you want, the closer you get to it, the more the powers-that-be might pull out the big guns to try and shake your composure or scare you into submission. Stand strong!

#11 Patience, young grasshopper

Change doesn't happen overnight. Rome was not built in a day. (And other sayings that mean the same thing.) Stick with it. Your cause is worth it.

#12 Inspire yourself

If you ever feel disillusioned or frustrated, revert to the greats:

'If I cannot do great things, I can do small things in a great way.' Martin Luther King

'I have never made but one prayer to God, a very short one: Oh Lord, make my enemies ridiculous. And God granted it.' Voltaire

'The first step is to establish that something is possible; then probability will occur.' Elon Musk

'I cannot say whether things will get better if we change; what I can say is that they must change if they are to get better.' Georg Lichtenberg

'Do not wait for leaders; do it alone, person to person.' Mother Theresa

#13 I get knocked down . . .

I've already mentioned (on page 7) that Rosa Parks trained as a civil rights activist. Well did you know that the NAACP (the National Association for the Advancement of Colored People) had already tried the same bus stunt three times before Rosa? For whatever reason it hadn't created the same stir that Rosa managed to do. Sometimes things fail: accept that now and agree you will keep on trying.

#14 Go tell it on a mountain

Stop saying 'no politics or religion at the dinner table'. We're sure whoever made that up is responsible for preventing millions of mini-revolutions. We must discuss our beliefs – firstly because how else will the message spread? But secondly because you need to hear any criticisms from close quarters. That way you can either tweak your campaign to solve them, or you can pre-empt what people at large will say and have your counter-arguments ready.

#15 Rules were made for breaking

Wanna know some rule breakers? Rifle through the history books and you'll spot them in governments the world over: the American Founding Fathers who overthrew British rule; the former president of Poland, Lech Walesa, who was arrested several times on his quest for workers' rights; Phoolan Devi, who killed the 22-strong group who gang-raped her and then was twice elected to the Indian Parliament – the list goes on. Now this is not a green card to do whatever you like. We here at *F**k the Establishment* headquarters don't advocate violence, and being peaceful and polite can be one of the most effective tools in your arsenal – offsetting against the bullying establishment you're up against. But equally don't be afraid of bending and breaking the rules. Sometimes defiance is what the world needs.

#16 Make like a CEO

Resistance should not be a mask for anger or complaining. Resistance should be a chance to take your anger and transform it into something magical. Get away from the mindset of knee-jerk protest. Yes, protest can work to help you get change, but it should be part of a larger strategy with goals and aims. Essentially you need to treat making change like a business. And that's what the next part of the book is all about . . .

TREAT CHANGE

LIKE BUSINESS

#17 Your goal

We asked you to write down your goal on page 2. Revisit it here. A goal shouldn't be so specific that the chances of involving other people in it are slim; a goal needs to be focused, but it should also be broad enough to make lots of people want to stand under its umbrella. Include other people in this conversation – you want your company to own the goal from the beginning and feel part of it so you can all spread the word more effectively.

#18 Your objectives

Because goals should be broad, they can also be a bit vague, and depending on how big and broad it is it might feel overwhelming. So break it down into achievable steps – realistic objectives that you can achieve. For example, if your goal is better services for young people in the community, what steps are going to get you there? Make your objectives 'SMART' – you might have had to do something similar if you have appraisals in your job. SMART stands for Specific, Measurable, Achievable, Realistic and Timely. For more advice on how to set these, www.projectsmart.co.uk offers a brilliant outline. Using these parameters to help you set the objectives for your goal will provide you with a clear focus and the beginnings of your strategy (discussed on pages 69–113).

#19 Put it on a Post-it

Review your objectives and be brutal with them – if two of them are similar, combine them. They should be as concise and to the point as possible: aim to have only three to five. Your goal and your objectives should all fit comfortably on a Post-it, which is convenient, because then you can carry it around with you wherever you go and continually stare at it to keep you focused.

#20 The business proposition

Your Post-it note agenda is for you and your company of like-minded people to internalise, but you should be prepared to expand on it when you present to the power. If you were going into a bank to apply for a business loan, you would (hopefully) go in prepared with all the records and plans you'd need to prove to the bank your business is worth the investment and that you'd be able to pay them back ASAP. You know what you want, but you also know what the bank needs to hear to give it to you. Think of your cause in the same way, through these next three steps . . .

#21 A) Do your homework

However much Donald Trump likes to ignore or dismiss facts, normal people will listen if you put easily digestible proof in front of them (or can get it in the hands of the media). If you want to change something, it will no doubt be because whatever's in place isn't working. Do you have the facts to back that up? If you don't, start collecting evidence or data to prove that. If you need facts, evidence, testimonies etc. – don't forget our good old friend the internet, who can be very helpful in collecting this. Make the facts specific and relatable to the power you're up against. Ideally show them how the issue conflicts with their values or promises they have made in the past – so you can assert that they're also personally in the wrong.

#22 B) Dangle the carrot

Don't just bring the stick! What good will your changes bring the power? Better social reputation? More engaged employees? Better results? Highlight what's in it for them and drive that home.

#23 C) The A to the B

Remember #3 Own the narrative? If you can, show the power what it's going to take to make the change happen, to prove to them that it's doable and to make the process seem as easy as possible.

#24 The elevator pitch

The business plan is for when you're in front of the power. You need to be able to summarise what you want and why you want it in a line for all and sundry who ask you. The snappier the better!

#25 Get a seat at the table

Repeat these words from Lin-Manuel Miranda's *Hamilton*: 'I want to be in the room where it happens' over and over to yourself. If you're not in the room where the decisions are happening, or at least talking to the people making the decisions, then you're not in charge of the change. You need to be in a position where you can negotiate.

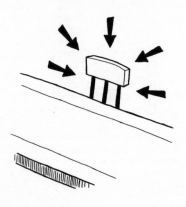

#26 Be prepared to compromise

Essentially: don't be a dick. Blind idealism won't get you anywhere. Work out what your red lines are and be prepared to negotiate on everything else. Make sure everyone in the group agrees with these so that when the time comes, negotiation can be just with the power and not among yourselves.

#27 Don't be fobbed off

Don't let anyone tell you it's not their problem. (I mean, sometimes it really isn't, so use your common sense here.) If the body you have beef with is your local school and they tell you that the issue doesn't lie with them, it lies with the local governing body, ask yourself if that's really true. If the school wants to come on side with you to take the issue up with the local governing body, that's great. If they don't, then is that because they're ducking responsibility? Will applying pressure on the school force their hand to resolve the problem with the local governing body?

#28 Be flexible

Any good business leader will tell you that you've got to be flexible. If a part of your campaign isn't working, or one of your objectives becomes impossible, change it. You're after change, after all, so you should be able to do it yourself! Keep reassessing the steps you've set out for yourself to make sure they're achievable – but also accept that change can take time.

#29 Evaluate

Every time you take action, set aside time to review what happened: what seemed to work the best? What didn't work? Is there anything off-strategy that you should quickly do now to capitalise on what's just happened? Keep notes of these things to help you in the future.

#30 The brains and the brawn

Businesses are more successful when they have diverse teams: a Harvard study showed that companies with diverse workforces are 45 per cent more likely to report market share growth from the previous year.[9] You want people working towards one goal but who can offer different perspectives, histories and skill sets. Don't recruit in an echo chamber; it's great to have numbers, and don't shut out anyone who wants in, but you also want numbers who can do different things: write well, speak well, research properly, charismatically talk to people, charismatically talk to another group of people, design placards, organise events, film videos, edit those videos, manage social media etc.

#31 Delegation

Micro-managing is a scourge upon the earth. Don't be that person. Hopefully you will pull together a group of people who have a huge range of different skills and talents. Some jobs you're going to be happy to hand over because you have no idea how to do them, other jobs you might rather do yourself because 'if you want something done right, you do it yourself'. Forget you know this phrase. Make everyone in your team feel useful or they won't keep coming back to help.

#32 Your brand is everything

Now at this point, we don't mean get out your felt-tips and draw a logo (although if you've got one up your sleeve then GREAT). What we do mean is have a good long think about how you're communicating your cause, both to the people you want to rally, and the power you're rallying against. Sam Conniff Allende in his terrific book *Be More Pirate* makes the point that it's no wonder so many people make unhealthy choices when advice about healthy attitudes is delivered in such a beige way, whereas campaigns for fizzy drinks and expensive trainers have so much thought and money pumped into them.[10] You might not have the money, but you can have the thought! Think about who your audience is and brand your cause accordingly.

#33 Money, money, money

We'd love to leave money out of it, but let's face it, like starting a business, change needs some financing – people need to travel places, you might need to hire event space, or provide food to encourage people to congregate. Be as clever as you possibly can with this – don't waste money on materials for placards if at home you're putting cardboard in the recycling bin, or on hiring a room for the group to meet if you're happy to do so in someone's front room. But there will likely be some things you need to fork out cash for, so ask everyone to bring with them one pound (or euro, or dollar etc.) every time you meet so you can start to build up a reserve. It's better to collect from the beginning than ask everyone to fork out twenty quid later on down the line.

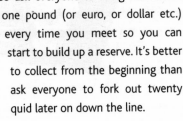

SAVE THE WORLD FUND

#34 Smoke and mirrors

Shout about your successes and the numbers behind you in a way that the power can't fail to see. Not only will this keep your tribe motivated, it's also going to put you on the map. Think about pirates' Jolly Roger flag – the skull and crossbones scared people so much many didn't even think about fighting back.[11]

#35 Always close the deal

The 'Strategise' section is going to give you ideas of how to apply pressure to get what you want. This might be petitions, marches, conferences or protests. Whatever you decide will work best, don't just do something splashy and then wait for the offer of negotiation to come to you. You need a campaign in place that is going to see you through to the very end of your objectives, and you need to keep applying pressure and following up until the deal is done.

45 Always close the deal

RALLY
___
THE
___
TROOPS

#36 Hi friends!

You can't do it alone and why would you want to? As we've already discussed, power can lie in numbers. They don't have to be big, just big enough to exert the pressure you need to achieve change, and as we discussed on page 43, ideally with a variety of skills that will get you to where you want to be. So time to get recruiting!

#37 Finding your tribe

Does a movement, charity or group tackling this issue already exist? Don't muddy the waters by creating a new tribe if they have the same aim as yours – instead go join them! If you have a slightly different aim but there are lots of similarities, can you talk to them about incorporating your aims? If no, then can you at least work together later down the line for more people power impact?

#38 Creating a tribe

Test the waters amongst your friends and ask if they'd like to join you – hopefully they in turn will have friends of friends who might be interested. Don't worry if your group is small. *Harry Potter* fans will remember that the sickly-sweet-but-also-evil Professor Umbridge banned meetings of students in groups of three or more during her time at Hogwarts – if she could feel threatened by protest groups of three, so will many other people in the Muggle world.

#39 Start where you are

Don't just talk to your friends. You will no doubt have another network: your company, your school/ university, your church. How can you tell everyone about your group? A big announcement would be great, but speaking individually to people usually has better results, especially if some of your network are a little shy. Can you recruit three or four other people in your network so that they in turn can try and recruit three or four people? A stone creates ripples!

#40 Don't be a hero

You don't need to be the beneficiary of the change: it's good to want good things for other people in your community. But you MUST have beneficiaries on board with what you're doing and involved in the process. Power can't be given, it must be taken, or you end up being part of the problem.

#41 Figureheads

As we discussed on the previous page, *you* don't need to be intrinsically linked to the change you want to see, but someone needs to be. Personal stories can count big-time in pulling on the power's heartstrings or the rest of the community's who you'd like to join the fight – don't underestimate their power. Make sure you have as many people with personal ties to the issue at stake as possible. One figurehead is great, but one figurehead and ten mini-figureheads is better.

#42 Unlikely friends

Don't just go after the people who you know are going to be friends to the cause. Don't go preaching or speaking to brick walls either, but try and get someone from the 'other side' to join the group. So for example, if the power you're up against is the local government, the ideal would be to get someone from the local government or someone who used to work there to join you. Then you can't be dismissed out of hand as merely busybodies or 'anti-government' — it opens your cause up and shows it's in the interest of more than just one group of people.

#43 Allies to the cause

Depending on what your cause is, work out if there are any other groups based nearby who might be able to back you and in return you'll back them. Ever watched the 2014 film *Pride*? It's based on a true story from the 80s, when a group of lesbian and gay activists fundraised for the British miners who were on strike at the time. This unlikely alliance led to hundreds of Welsh miners joining the fight for gay rights.

#44 Be inclusive

Lots of people don't identify as being political. Ask yourself why that is. It might be because as soon as anyone talks about protests or politics or activism they imagine someone who doesn't look like them: someone opinionated, or aggressive, or cheerleadery. So take the politics out of it – make it purely about the change you want to see. And make the process fun – bring in social elements, don't let it get cliquey. Go outside to find people, approach people personally; don't expect people to just find you.

#45 Be the parent

Whilst we're being inclusive, accept that some people are going to be divisive. If you find you've got a divisive (*cough* annoying) person in the group, privately tell them to cut it out. You don't want them to put everyone else in the group off.

#46 Unite your troops

Make everyone feel part of the conversation. Let everyone introduce themselves and give each person time to speak on the topic. It's going to be important to find out what makes the power tick (see page 72), but it's also important to find out what makes your troops tick so that you can ensure the campaign is consistently relevant to them. Find the common ground around the cause – why is everyone interested in it? What's fuelling them? Make a note of everyone's skills and stories as they talk.

#47 FaceTime

Once you've got your core group striving for change, at one point or another you might need to pull in some more numbers for support. Social media and the internet are terrific at spreading petitions, crowdsourcing and notifying people about events or protests i.e. the short-attention-span things. They're not very good at making a person identify with something wholly, folding them into a cause, or listening to their opinions. If you really want a campaign to be long-lasting, you need to get out and talk – and listen – to people and build a relationship with them.

#48 Make it fun

When you're taking the issue out to a wider audience, don't assume everyone will care as much as you do. For some issues, people are so invested that they're going to make the time to come no matter what. But for others – people who are at school or work all day, who have kids to put to bed and chores to complete – getting people together is tricky. So make it worth their while – make it a tea party or offer pizza and drinks, and do it at times that people will actually be able to make. Hold it in a location that people can easily get to – if you're at a university, can you all meet in the library café during lunch? Or a location that's central to everyone or on their way home from lectures?

I'm saving the world!

#49 Celebrate good times

Motivation is so key to making change. There's only so far anger is going to get you. Every little win you have – celebrate it.

#50 Hope is the good stuff

Norwegian politician Per Espen Stoknes gave a cracking TED talk in 2017 on how to transform apocalypse fatigue into action on global warming. The big takeaway? Humans don't like doom, they like hope. So whatever your cause, don't use the doom of the situation to bring people together – use the hope of the solution. William H. McRaven in his bestselling book *Make Your Bed* says, 'We will all find ourselves neck deep in mud someday. That is the time to sing loudly, to smile broadly, to lift up those around you and give them hope that tomorrow will be a better day.'[12] Amen, brother.

#51 Take talking seriously

Take any speeches you write seriously because they can make a big difference to getting people on side. Watch TED talks or politicians' speeches to inspire you and jot down what works best. Also think back to any lessons you had about writing speeches in school (finally a chance to put what you learnt in class to good use!). You want clarity; emotive stories that are backed up by facts; an ending that connects with your beginning; alliteration or 'triples' if relevant; a fat lump of hope (see previous page) etc. Go make your teacher proud.

STRATEGISE

#52 Think small to think big

You've got your goal, your objectives, your troops – now it's time to work out how to make your objectives a reality. Making all the steps from here on out as small as possible is absolutely key. Mother Theresa once said, about the people she helped in Calcutta, 'If I'd never have picked up the first person, I'd never have picked up the 42,000.' Like Mother Theresa, don't just do one small thing. Decide which small things are going to achieve your objectives and assemble them into a plan of action. And don't forget to assign the right person or people to carry these small steps out, including everyone in your team as you go.

#53 Identify who has the power

Working out what steps are going to best achieve your objectives depends on who makes the decisions surrounding your cause. Is it one person or a group of people? How easy is it to get to that person or group of people? Depending on your cause, the person or people with the power might be quite high up, in which case, who reports to the power/ who does he/she/they depend on? Is there a forum where issues similar to yours are discussed i.e. is that where you need to get to? These are all questions you need the answers to in order to decide how to progress.

#54 Keep your friends close . . .

Once you know who holds the power, build a picture of them to help shape your campaign. If your cause is about school and the power has children of school age, that's useful to know when trying to get them to sympathise with your cause. Before deciding on external pressure or people power tactics, try to build a relationship with the power. Remember what we discussed on page 17 – your opponent is not a Disney villain. They think and feel too and therefore might have strings you can pull before having to go down a bigger road. If for whatever reason you can't build a

relationship with them – maybe you've never met them, maybe they're ignoring your emails – find someone who does have a relationship with them, and see if you can get them on board with your change.

#55 Timing is key

As any comedian knows, it's all about timing. Is there an ideal time to put your issue on the table? If it's a local community issue, the run-up to local government elections is going to be a time when politicians are very willing to listen. Equally, are there times when starting a campaign would be pointless? If you're at university, starting once exams are over might seem like a good idea because that's when students are less busy. But they're also more likely to be looking ahead to the summer holidays at this point (and potentially more interested in partying). Would the first term, in the run-up to Christmas, work better, when people have that back-to-school fervour and aren't bogged down with revision?

#56 Inside pressure approach

Are there any creative ways you can make change from the inside? In 2003, a London cleaner earning £4.50 an hour connected with enough other people to become a shareholder in the building he cleaned: the HSBC headquarters. It meant he had a seat at the table at the annual general meeting of the bank, and he made a speech to the chairman of the bank telling him how hard it was to provide for his family off that wage. The story was covered in the papers and within 18 months HSBC had increased the wage of its cleaners. Are there any internal pressure points you can manipulate too?

#57 Outside pressure approach

The following few pages will you give ideas on how to approach getting what you want through bringing the issue to the power's attention and then applying some good old-fashioned peer pressure: if you can get lots of people to vocalise their agreement for the cause, the power will have to give in. How many people you need to apply pressure is going to be relative to the body of power you're up against, so think about this carefully. Use that load of common sense you were born with, too: you might not need to do all of these steps, you might need to do more or you might think of ways to be more creative – in which case more power to you!

#58 Aim below the target

First off, seed the campaign in with the people around and directly below whoever holds the power. Can you get anyone on side who has good links to the power? In 2014 and 2015, Avaaz worked hard to get over 30 cabinet ministers and world leaders to join their People's Climate Marches: a real coup. How can you do that for your cause? Who is slightly further down the chain but is still in the line of command? Even if they don't want to join the group – which is the ideal – having them on side will count in your favour so start the conversation at this lower level first.

#59 Contact the power

Write a letter or an email (something in writing) setting out what the issue is and what you want them to do about it. Make your argument compelling but short and put facts and evidence (page 34) and your speech skills (page 67) to good use here. Get all the people in your group to sign it. The ideal would be the power then replies saying 'sure thing, we'll put plans in place to make that change right away.' The reality is you might not hear back from them, or they might try to fob you off. Do NOT be fobbed off (page 40).

#60 Take 2

If you didn't hear back from the power, write a similar letter to your previous one, stating the original letter's date and that you are waiting for a response. Get more people to sign this letter than you did before.

#61 Time to discuss

Hopefully at this point, depending on the cause and the size of your support relative to it, the power will invite you to discuss the issues and configure a solution. Great! Don't forget to a) not be fobbed off (page 40) but also b) that you should be willing to compromise (page 39). But if you don't get a reply, it's time to get more people involved ...

#62 Power to the petition

You may have five people in your group, you may have twenty-five. Each of you will have your own network of friends, families and colleagues. Enlist their help. Start a petition and get everyone you know and more to sign it. Try as hard as you can to get people the power will recognise to sign it too – the ones you identified back on page 76. And if you're really, really serious, don't forget the power of getting everyone to share the petition using social media.

#63 Write one more letter

Include copies of your previous two letters and explain that you now have a petition with however many signatures you've collected. Then do something creative with that petition – get the local press to print it, email it to every person in the body of power you're up against, share the results on social media – whatever you think will make the biggest splash depending on your cause, the audience and who the power is. In this example, let's say you tell the power that you look forward to delivering it in person with those people who signed the petition standing behind you. If you want to be polite you can include the date you'll be delivering it, but depending who you're up against, you might then find your way barred (although melodrama on their part can play into your hands – think of the Twitter storm!).

#64 Deliver your petition in person

Engage some peaceable people power! The amount of people you need to help you deliver the petition should be relative to the body of power you're up against. If the body of power is the government, then to make them take notice, you're going to need a lot of people standing behind you when you deliver that petition (in which case you're looking at more of a protest, pages 85-94). But if it's a company, the local government or a school, then work out how many people standing behind you is going to make a difference; it might be fifty, it might be one hundred and fifty — make sure it's doable, but believe in yourself that it definitely will be.

#65 Invite the local media along

Be clever in how you do this. Make it something they'll want to cover. Talk to them when they arrive and try to get them on side. Sell them personal stories and introduce them to your figurehead(s) if that's not you, or whoever has the most compelling reason to be there. You might decide your peaceable walk should include some signage. If it does, think about the audience of the local media; will any of the slogans alienate them or be too rude to include in photographs? If you can't get the local media along, remember your good old friend social media! Get everyone to continually share what's going on.

#66 Aftermath

The idea is that the amount of people pressure you've applied will make the power sit up and take you seriously so talks can begin. Again remember to not be fobbed off (page 40), but that you also need to compromise (page 39). If you're not given a seat at the table at this point, you need to figure out why: is it that your objectives aren't realistic enough? Is it that you haven't applied enough people pressure? What would apply *more* pressure? Is there a different public arena you can try the issue in? Is there a way of getting the power to care more? There are plenty more options to try!

#67 How to protest

A good protest as part of a proper campaign can go a long way, especially if you have the numbers on your side. 1.5 million people marched in the People's Climate Marches in 2014 and 2015, proving to governments around the world that people cared. That's what protests are good for: making statements. They're not that good at making tangible change in and of themselves. After the marches, the work continued to lobby governments to make commitments and put policies in place. Over the next few pages you'll find some tips on how to organise a protest – just remember it is only part of the journey towards change; that you still need a goal, objectives, an established relationship with the powers-that-be, and the motivation to make the aim of your protest stick!

#68 Legal bits

First things first, don't forget that in lots of countries, you need a permit to protest legally. Do your research before you start organising to find out what hoops you need to jump through

#69 Location, location

Ideally you need a place to meet and a place to end up, so that you can all walk together to your finish line and cause more of a stir. The places you pick need to be big enough for you to congregate, but hopefully not so big that your protesting party will look small. Make it convenient for your group to get to, but also remember there's no point going to protest outside a building that has nothing to do with the cause – where you protest should be symbolic as well as practical.

#70 Time

If the majority of your protesters work weekdays, don't make the protest Thursday at 2pm – do it after work or at the weekend. The only caveat to that is if your cause is against a company or local government that DOES work during the week: then ideally there will be some overlap of your protest and their working hours to make the biggest impact on the body you're protesting against. Don't just decide on a start time, also decide on an end time – you don't want the protest to just tail off or disband because there's nothing left to do. The next page will help you with this.

#71 Organised fun

If you've been to a protest before you know that it's not just turn up, march, on your bike. There's a proper community spirit that is fired up by an opening talk, various other speeches by notable names and maybe even live music. If you expect a big crowd, you need a stage. If you expect a REALLY big crowd, it might even be worth having two so that the people further back aren't left out. Make sure enough of the organisers also have loud speakers so that they can start motivational chants. Also decide how you're going to end your protest – what's the final note you want to finish on?

#72 Come one, come all!

Once all your ducks are in a row, it's time to spread the word! While social media seems like the obvious choice, how you do this depends entirely on your audience. If you're targeting the local community, do they have a website or a Facebook group? If groups run in the local village or town hall, can you ask the teachers or leaders to tell everyone about the upcoming protest? Can you and your group of comrades go door-to-door to tell people why it's important? Whilst so many people seem to be up for a bit of protest, lots of people don't believe in its power any more, so explaining the wider campaign around the protest and your aims face-to-face can be really beneficial. And if you convince one person wholeheartedly, they're likely to bring a friend, or their family, or spread the word for you.

#73 Read all about it!

Invite the media – local or otherwise. Once you have a rough idea of how many people are going to come (be conservative here: divide the numbers of people who have said yes by two at least), invite the media again, quoting the number you think will show to prove that it's going to be a big deal. Better yet, get someone from the media to join your group so you have guaranteed coverage. And don't forget social media – create a hashtag and continually remind people throughout the day to share what's going on using it.

#74 Accessorise

You might want to take signs that are eye-catching, funny or provocative. (Remember what we said on page 83 about the media, though – you can't stop other people bringing rude signs but maybe don't carry one yourself if it's going to put a journalist off.) You also might want to think about asking everyone to wear something – the protesters against oil taxes and President Macron's government in France in 2018-2019 wore yellow vests, serving to both single themselves out from other Parisians and to unite themselves as one unit with one voice. Elsewhere, marchers on the International Day to End Violence Against Sex Workers (17 December) carry red umbrellas to draw attention to their campaign.

#75 Making the most of it

Devote enough of your group to talking to as many people who have turned up as possible. If attendants don't know the wider aims of the protest, ask them if they'd like to know more about it. Would they be happy to give you their email address so you can keep them up-to-date with the campaign's progress? Would they like to join your group meetings? Why is it that they're marching today – do they have a particular affiliation with the cause that would be useful to add to any data you want to present to the powers-that-be? You've managed to get all these people in one place – try as hard as you can to make as many of them feel as involved and important as possible, and to keep them as involved and important as possible as you go forwards.

#76 Aftermath

Your organisation was tip-top, your turn-out was wondrous, your speakers were eloquent and everyone has gone home feeling elated. Now it's time to keep that momentum going. Contact the power again with a round-up of the protest to drive home how many people marched and how invested they are in the cause. Hopefully the power will want to sit down and negotiate with you, but if they don't, don't give up. Review your objectives, try to reach out to other people around the power that you haven't tried before, or give one or several of the ideas over the next few pages a go.

actual finish line

FINISH

#77 Strikes

Strikes can sometimes feel un-rebellious because in most countries, workforces have to first get permission to do so. Sort of like a child asking permission to refuse to go to bed. However, don't rule strikes out as ineffective! They can cause a lot of disruption, which can force the power's hand to give you a seat at the table to negotiate. An example of one such successful strike was when the UK postal workforce, worried about job security due to incoming modernisation plans, held a number of strikes between 2009 and 2010. It meant tens of millions of items were undelivered and forced the bosses to, ahem, *strike* a deal with them. Strikes depend on you having something to withhold that will irritate the power, or the populace or both. If that's you, it might be worth considering.

#78 Boycotts

Boycotting buying products, or using a service, or trading with someone can also be an effective way of making the powers-that-be listen to your demands. However, bear in mind that depending on who you're up against, you need a lot of people to make a difference and you need them to maintain that boycott for a sustained period of time. Probably the most famous of all boycotts was the Montgomery Bus Boycott in 1955 that Rosa Parks sparked – it worked, but the boycott lasted 381 days. But don't let that put you off; it was a boycott of British salt that marked a turning point in Gandhi's struggle for Indian independence too – so if you're up to the challenge, you're walking in illustrious footsteps.

#79 Walk-outs

Depending on your cause, this could be a really creative way of making the power take note. It's essentially a mini-strike, but if you can get everyone to do it at exactly the same time, then it can cause a big stir. On top of this, strikes usually only work for a big labour force, whereas walk-outs can be used by various groups of people. Imagine if you could get everyone to get up and walk out of a theatre in the middle of a show at exactly the same time, or walk out of a school – imagine if you could get several schools to do it. So long as the powers-that-be are close by enough to see it, or enough people are there to report on it or share it online, the organisation of it will definitely unnerve the power enough to sit up and take note.

#80 Seeing is believing

The best PR campaigns are as focused as they are broad – focused in that the coverage is featured in media the audience for the product consume; broad in that it covers as many media outlets within that framework as possible. Think about it – when a big Hollywood film comes out, you suddenly start seeing the lead on covers of magazines, in newspaper interviews, on TV chat shows – the list goes on. How can we get a piece of that for ourselves? If your cause is a local community issue, then could you display something that relates to your cause in as many houses and buildings as possible? If you have a mantra or a logo, or you chose to protest with a particular item, could you go door-to-door and ask people to display it as big as possible in the windows of their homes? Be targeted about it – doing this will advertise your cause to more people and hopefully encourage them to be involved, but ideally it would be in a place the power lives or has to drive through each day so that they're also exposed to it.

#81 The human chain

A creative way to draw attention to your campaign is by forming a human chain. In 1986, Hands Across America brought 6.5 million people together, including many celebrities and President Reagan, to form a human chain to raise money for charities whose mission was to prevent hunger and homelessness. Participants were supposed to donate $10 each – this wasn't quite achieved but the campaign still raised an incredible $34 million. Similarly in 1989, two million hands joined together to form a human chain that went through Estonia, Latvia and Lithuania to protest for independence from the USSR (which was ultimately successful in 1991).

#82 Can you blog it? Yes you can!

Think about what free internet tools you have at your disposal that could help your cause. One you might settle on is blogging. There are an estimated 4.5 million blogs already in existence so you've got a lot of competition, but that shouldn't stop you if you think there's an audience or you have a viewpoint to offer that's different from any others you can find. The extraordinary woman that is Malala Yousafzai started a blog in 2009 about girls' rights to education, which in turn meant *The New York Times* made a documentary about her life as the Pakistani military's presence grew in and around where she lived. Malala's blog was for BBC Urdu – so blogging from an already established platform would be the ideal. But equally, if you have a good network who all agree to continually and consistently share the blog to their online followers, you could build a platform of your own.

#83 Events

Throwing a fun event can raise awareness for a campaign and allow an opportunity to gather more supporters, more data and more positive coverage. (And possibly some funds too!) Have a think about what that event could be: a village fete, a car boot sale, a carol concert, a mini music festival, a mass dog walk – something that would appeal to your audience but also be an opportunity for you to do the above.

#84 Man's best friend

Not dogs sadly — our new, less cuddly best friend: TECHNOLOGY. Specifically, how you can use technology to make your aim more digestible to your audience and make them more likely to spread it. Depending on who your audience is, videos can be a brilliant option — if you can put together something impassioned, or poignant or funny depending on what is most likely to appeal. Another idea might be a meme or a gif; something short and funny that people are very likely to share.

#85 Conversations with friends

Can you get the power or someone close to the power in a room, on a stage to talk about the issue at hand? That can be a brilliant opportunity to back them into a corner with emotive stories and facts and force their hand to commit to change.

#86 The law

Certain types of media want you to believe that lawyers aren't on your side, but there's a lot of power in the law. Depending on what your cause is or what power you're up against, don't discount the law as being an amazing tool in getting what you want. In Matthew Bolton's blinder of a book *How to Resist* he talks about how ClientEarth took the British government to court – and won – because they didn't meet their existing legal obligations to reduce pollution. There are lots of

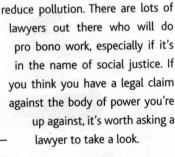

lawyers out there who will do pro bono work, especially if it's in the name of social justice. If you think you have a legal claim against the body of power you're up against, it's worth asking a lawyer to take a look.

#87 PR stunts

Explore what PR stunts have worked in the past and why – not just in the realms of campaigning but for consumer products. Be creative depending on what your cause demands – don't do it just for the sake of it, remember it needs to be effective against who the power is or in raising awareness, or ideally both. Taylor Herring have a great blog post on their website about the top 50 PR stunts if you're looking for some inspiration.

#88 Capitalise on trends

Can you tie in a PR stunt or one of the other ideas above with a trend or something that's happening in the media right now? A brilliant recent example is the way women across America, Canada and Argentina have dressed up as handmaids from *The Handmaid's Tale* against anti-abortion laws and misogynistic healthcare bills, following the adaptation of Margaret Atwood's book into a TV series. Using such a widely recognised symbol of female oppression – the fictional Handmaid's costume – received worldwide attention.

#89 Press releases

Don't underestimate how useful these can be. If your cause relates to a certain industry, or a certain community, then a well-placed press release detailing your campaign or a particular newsworthy event within it to relevant media might get word out to someone you haven't had a chance to speak to, but who might be really passionate about what you're doing.

#90 Social media's superpowers

Social media can be ephemeral for sure and it might not be able to cement meaningful relationships, but that doesn't mean it doesn't have its uses. Play to its strengths. For example, use social media to share and document events, and encourage people to sign petitions. Use Twitter to connect with like-minded individuals who have big followings, and create Facebook groups when you're talking to smaller audiences who you know spend time on the site (which is actually most people, although it's particularly useful if you're targeting 25–34-year-olds).[13]

#91 Learn from history

The age-old adage which humans have never actually paid much attention to, but now you can prove them wrong! Hopefully the ideas within this section have provided you with plenty of inspiration, but make sure you do your research into previous campaigns for change, big and small, and note down what's worked for them to give you ideas for your own campaign. We've done our own digging and have catalogued a few case studies you might find interesting over the next few pages.

#92 Case study 1

The famous campaign for civil rights in Birmingham, Alabama in 1963 had its stumbling points but ultimately its victories. It is an excellent example of the leaders of that campaign understanding the power they were up against — knowing the sheriff's department was intensely racist, and afraid of change, and would do anything to break up the protest. The police department eventually used fire hoses and dogs to try to disperse protesters and this extreme action caught the attention of the rest of the country and the world, forcing a civil rights bill to be passed. The lesson? Understand the power you're up against, push their buttons if necessary, and use defeat and overreaction to your advantage.

#93 Case study 2

Back in the 60s, the only radio that existed in Britain did not cater to a mass audience (think classical music and government-approved news items). With the government refusing to incorporate anything new, a 'pirate' radio called Radio Caroline started transmitting on a boat in international waters off the south coast of England. (If this is all sounding familiar, it might be because you watched *The Boat That Rocked* – the cracking 2009 film starring Philip Seymour Hoffman and Bill Nighy.) This sparked numerous more pirate radio stations over the next few years, and whilst the government cracked down hard, eventually they had to concede to more choice on official radio. Why? Because a third of the population was listening to the pirate radio stations, which in turn meant advertisers were taking their business there. What can we learn from this? Circumventing the rules can work if there's enough people power behind it.

#94 Case study 3

The Singing Revolution describes the events that led to Estonia, Latvia and Lithuania's independence from the USSR, so-called because it was kicked off by large groups of people singing forbidden national songs and hymns in public, including a 300,000-strong mass demonstration in Tallinn. The fight for independence for the Baltic States took four years, so lesson one is, as ever, stick at it! But the second lesson is how much power something as simple as singing held — not only did it motivate the Estonian people, it was an attractive story for the rest of the world to cover.

#95 Case study 4

In November 2018, thousands of people gathered across five bridges in central London because of the looming climate change crisis — without permission: what's known as 'civil disobedience'. They were purposely flouting the rules because, in the words of one of the organisers, Gail Bradbrook, 'The "social contract" has been broken . . . [and] it is therefore not only our right but our duty to bypass the government's inaction and flagrant dereliction of duty and to rebel to defend life itself.'[14] How successful this will be as part of wider climate change campaigns is yet to be seen, but what we should take away is that they didn't just flout the rules for the sake of it, they flouted the rules because it made sense to their campaign. Messaging is key.

FINAL

THINGS TO

THINK ABOUT

#96 Be a problem solver

Depending on what the problem is, do you really need the Establishment to fix it? Can you do something about it yourself? In Britain, the pressure on the National Health Service (NHS) is huge. One doctors' surgery in Croydon identified that people were coming to them with issues the NHS couldn't treat because the problems weren't solvable through pills. They resolved to do something about it by linking up with the wider community. They started a scheme loosely called 'social prescribing', where doctors recommended to patients different activities such as exercise and cooking classes, gardening, counselling, and administrative support. Through this they've helped people take their wellness and happiness into their own hands and have prevented illnesses, rather than just treating them – something that has not only helped their patients but taken pressure off the NHS services.

#97 Rewrite the rule book

In your quest for change, has it made you feel frustrated about the current hierarchy? If yes, then how do you want the hierarchy of tomorrow to look? Is this your next cause?! Divisive as he might be, channel some Elon Musk – imagine the world as you want to see it and go get it; don't feel constrained by the rules that were forced upon you by the Establishment before you were even born.

#98 If you can't beat 'em . . .

Okay, so hear us out. Politics is a bit of a dirty word right now, huh? But if this book is trying to make one point, it's that change is always possible. We're always going to have politicians ruling the country, so if you don't like the way they do things, change them. Be the change you want to see, and all that. Sometimes the only way you can drive change is by being on the inside of a system, so don't rule it out. And don't fob your*self* off – don't believe that nothing will ever change. The sheer amount of change that has got us to this point in time is huge, so why can't things change again?

#99 You're not alone

If there's one way to feel automatically engaged in campaigning for change it's by signing up to Avaaz, the online campaigning community we mentioned back on page 5. The amount of campaigns that community has successfully contributed to after just five years is staggering, and it campaigns in 15 languages across six continents so is open to the whole world. Become one of its 50 million members today and feel automatically part of some people power.

#100 Start now

Nothing good ever happened from sitting still. The greatest enemy of change is inactivity. If you have a cause, don't wait. Start rallying your troops and strategising today. You're off to great places, as Dr Seuss says, so be on your way.[15]

#101 Pass it on

This book has (hopefully) been a champion for people power: showcasing how utterly incredible, and oftentimes unstoppable, people can be when they stand shoulder to shoulder against the Establishment. So now we've come to the end, there's only one thing left to do: turn to the person sitting next to you on the bus, or your friend sitting beside you in the library, or knock on your neighbour's door, and hand them this here book. If knowledge is power, let's share it.

REFERENCES

1   According to Milton Leitenberg, Roberto Muehlenkamp, 'How many people died in all the wars in the 20th century', www.quora.com (8 January 2017).
2   Sarah O'Connor, 'Millennials poorer than previous generations, data show', www.ft.com (23 February 2018).
3   'Impact', www.change.org (accessed 3 February 2019).
4   'Our Victories', www.avaaz.org (accessed 3 February 2019).
5   Alan Bennett, *The History Boys* (London, 2004).
6   'Democracy', en.oxforddictionaries.com (accessed 3 February 2019).
7   Sam Conniff Allende, *Be More Pirate* (London, 2018).
8   Quote from Swami Sivananda, a Hindu spiritual teacher in the first half of the twentieth century.
9   Sylvia Ann Hewlett, Melinda Marshall and Laura Sherbin, 'How Diversity Can Drive Innovation', *Harvard Business Review* (Harvard, 2013).
10 Sam Conniff Allende, *Be More Pirate* (London, 2018).
11 Ibid.
12 William H. McRaven, *Make Your Bed* (London, 2017).
13 Katie Sehl, 'All the Facebook Demographics That Matter to Social Media Marketers', blog.hootsuite.com (28 May 2018).
14 Quote taken from an article written by Matthew Taylor and Damien Gayle, 'Dozens arrested after climate protest blocks five London bridges', www.theguardian.com (17 Nov 2018).
15 Dr. Seuss, *Oh, the Places You'll Go!* (London, 2003).